Take Me to School
by Nancy Hanna

Copyright © 2015 Nancy Hanna

All rights reserved.

ISBN: **1512174807**
ISBN-13: **978-1512174809**

DEDICATION

Chris, Dylan, and Laura

I need to be in school every day unless I am sick.

You may think I am just playing, but play is how I learn.

Every day attendance helps me have a schedule and routine.

I am learning important skills to get ready for school.

I am learning to have friends and be a friend.

I am learning to control my emotions.

I am learning the building blocks for future reading and math skills.

Help me learn that school matters.
Every day.

Help me be on time for school.

My teachers and friends miss me when I am absent.

I can draw a picture of myself at school.

For parents:

Did you know….

- Absenteeism in the first month of school can predict poor attendance throughout the school year. Half the students who miss 2-4 days in September go on to miss nearly a month of school.
- Poor attendance in pre-k through second grade can influence whether children read proficiently by the end of third grade or be held back.
- By 6th grade, chronic absence becomes a leading indicator that a student will drop out of high school.
- Research shows that missing 10 percent of the school year, or about 18 days in most school districts, negatively affects a student's academic performance. That's just two days a month and that's known as chronic absence.
- The academic impact of missing that much school is the same whether the absences are excused or unexcused.
- When students improve their attendance rates, they improve their academic prospects and chances for graduating.

Attendance Works. (2014). Retrieved May 13, 2015.

About the author:

Nancy Hanna taught at the elementary, middle, and high school levels for more than twenty years. She was a middle school principal for three years. She currently serves as Early Childhood Director for Greenbrier County Schools in West Virginia. She lives in White Sulphur Springs, WV

Made in United States
Troutdale, OR
02/26/2024